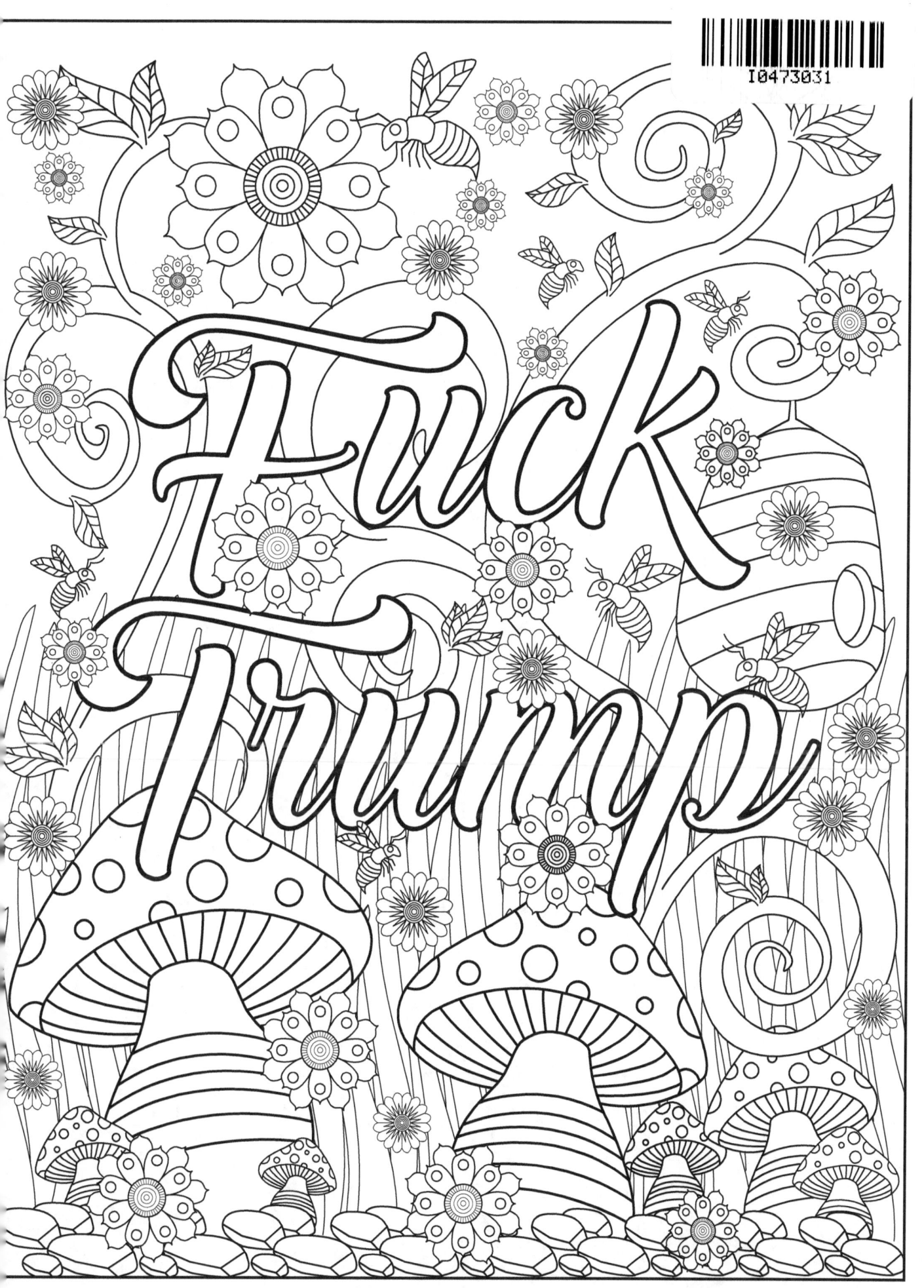

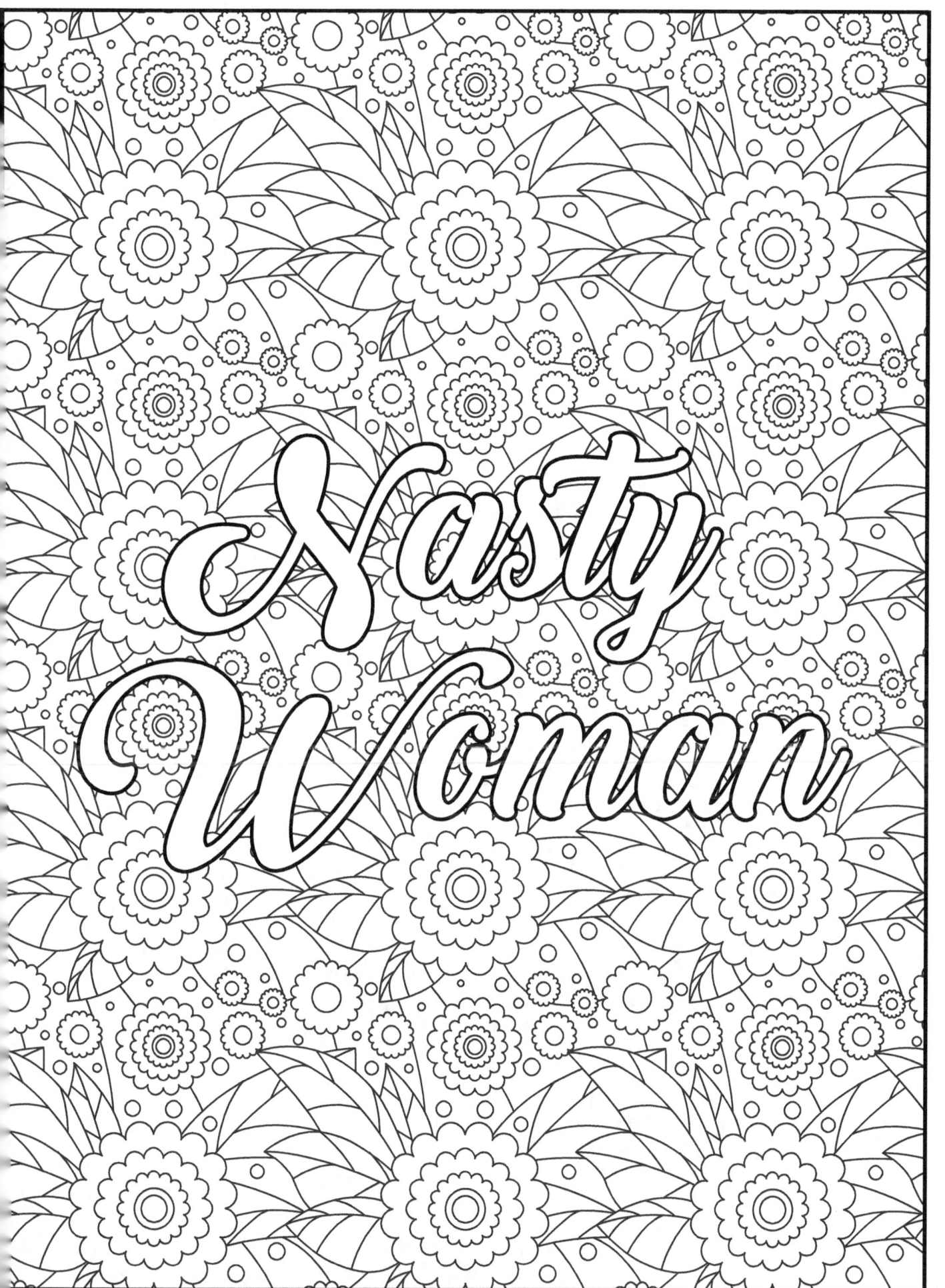

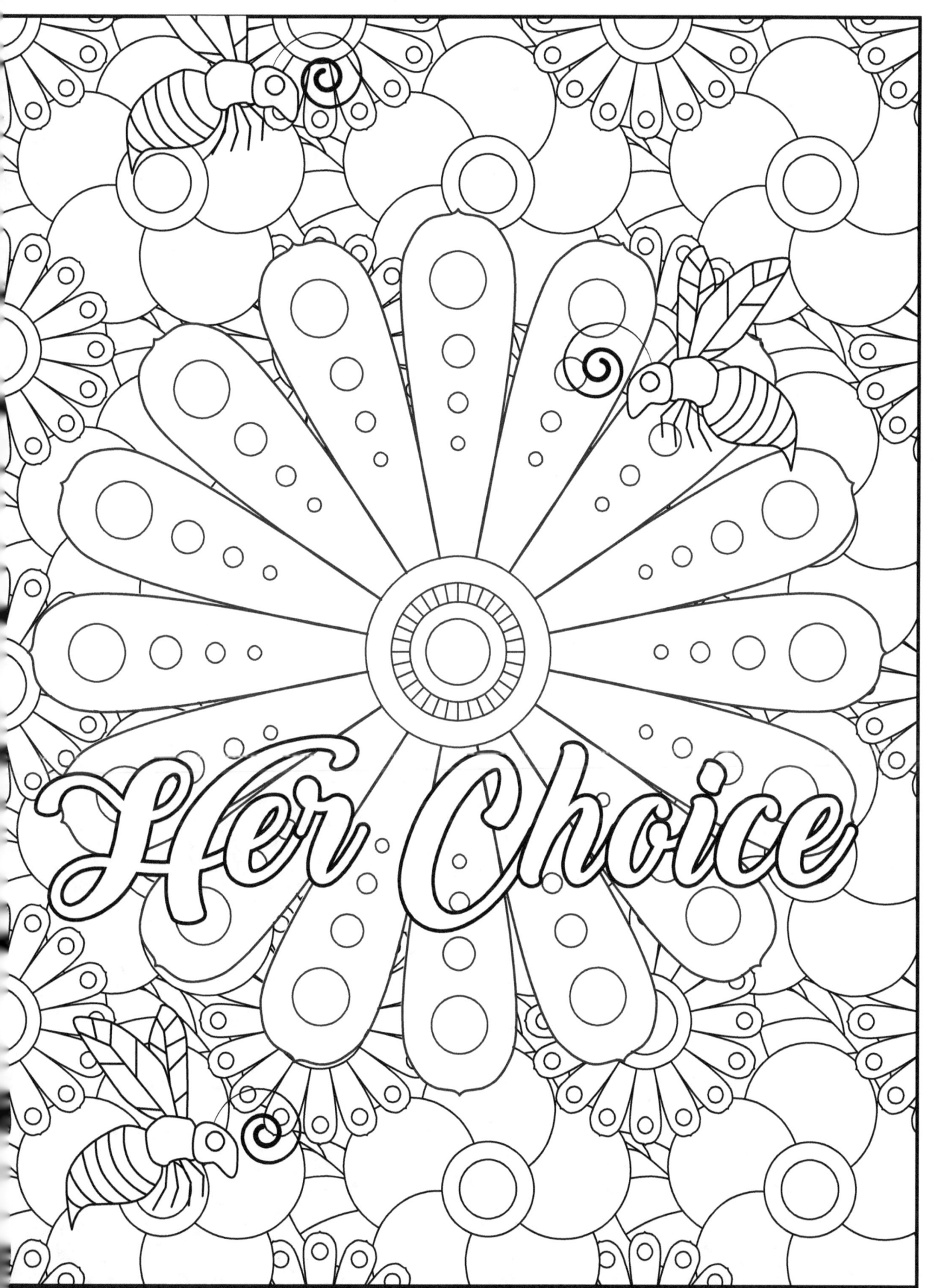

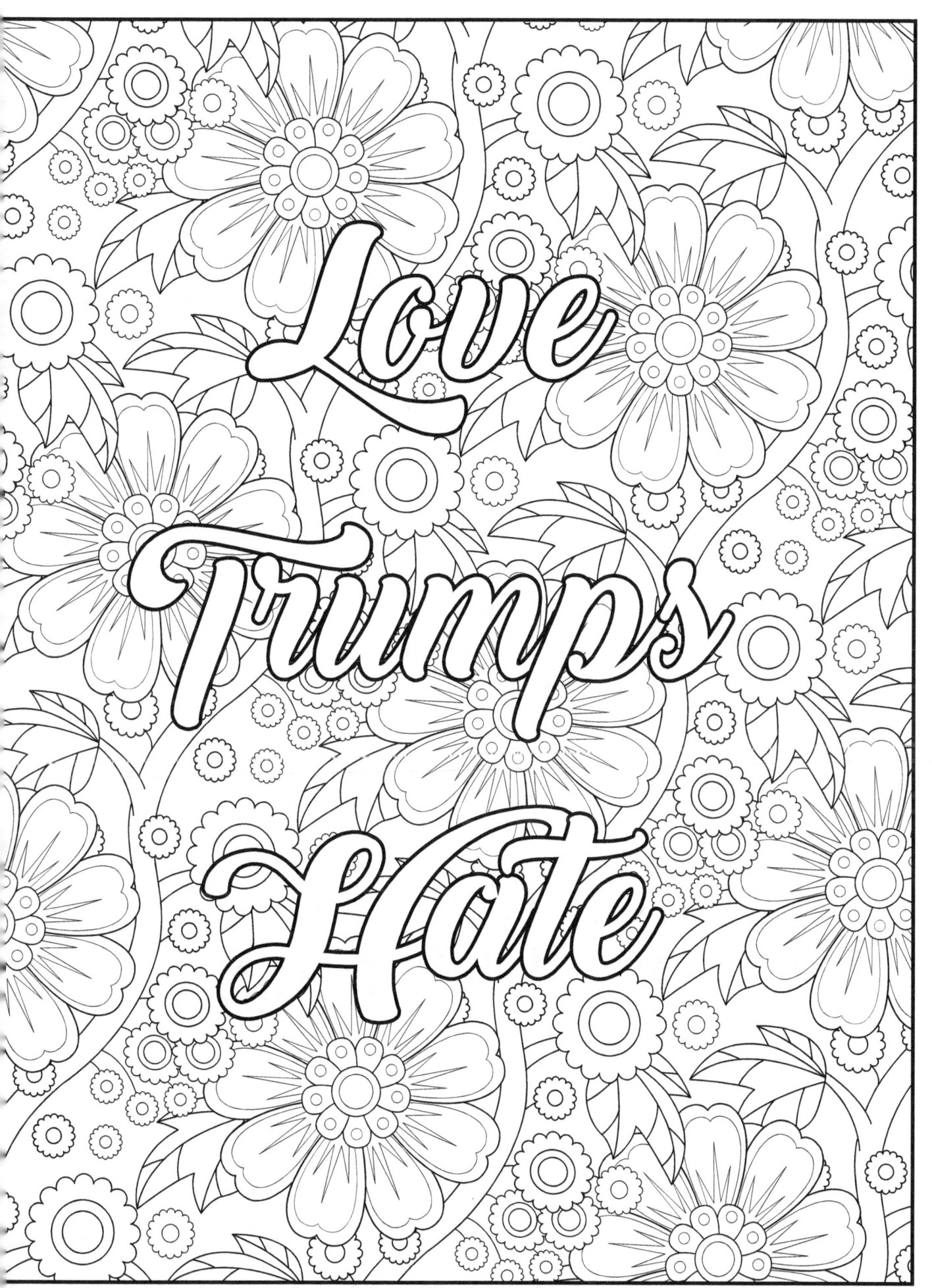

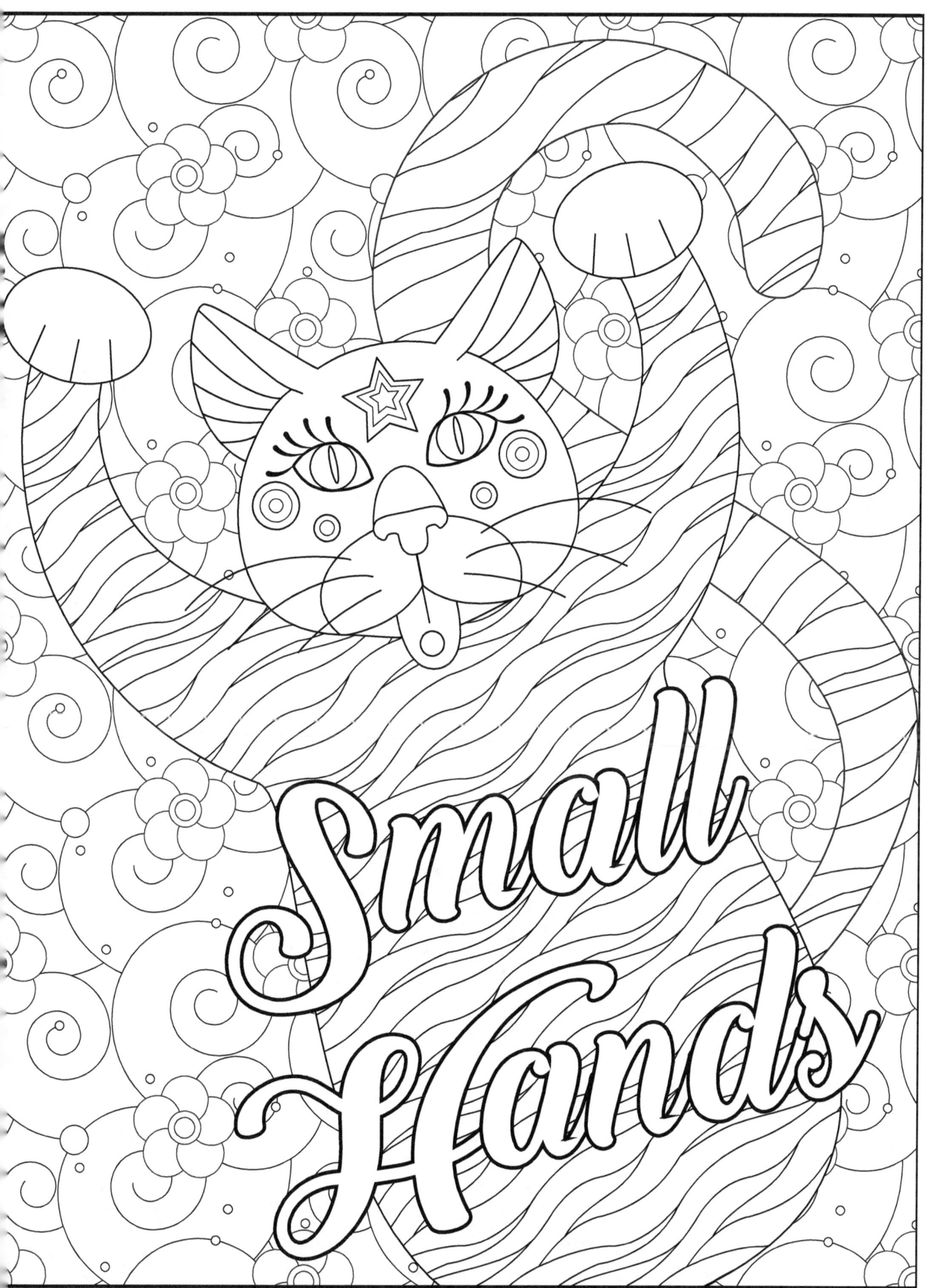

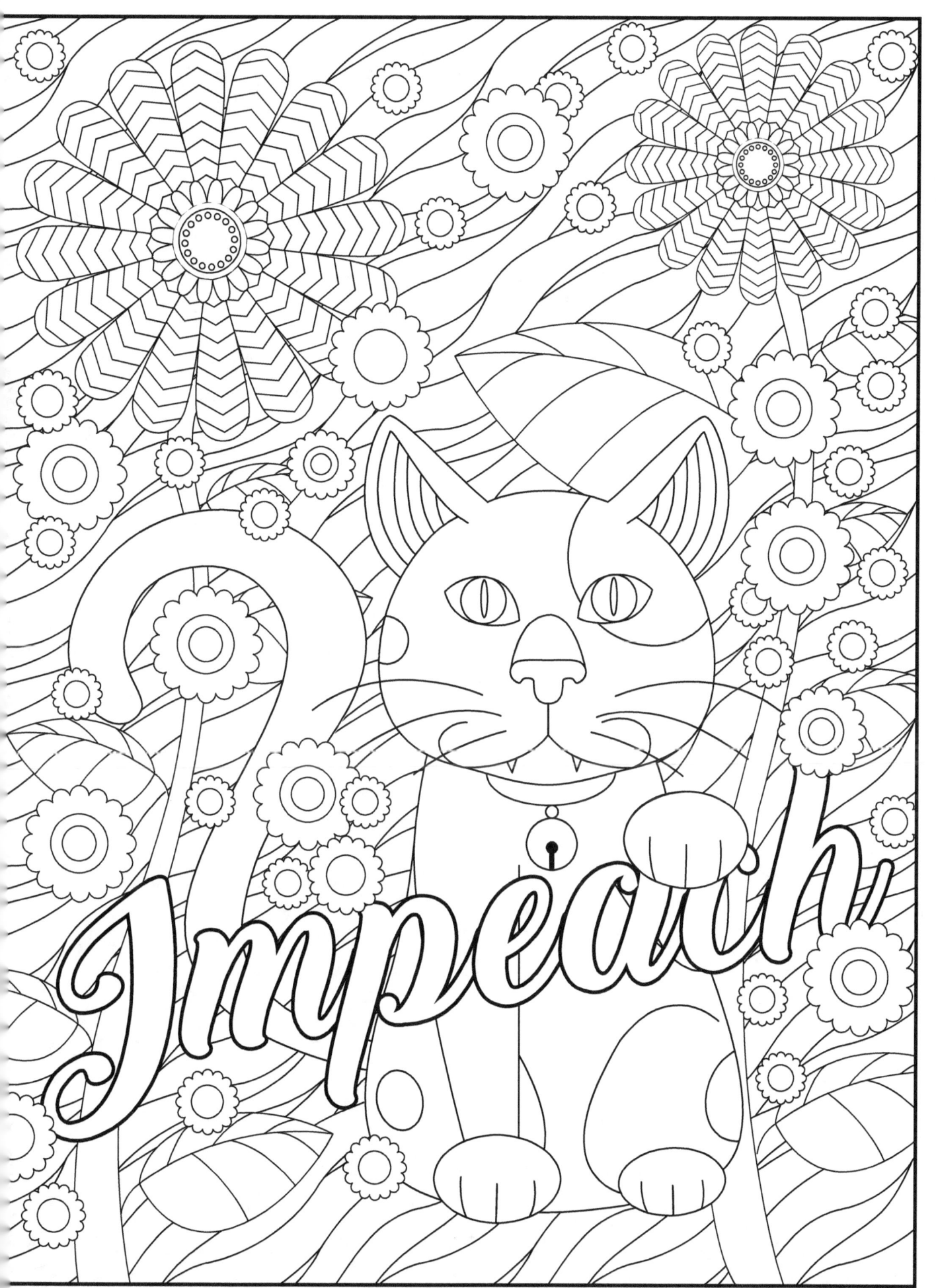

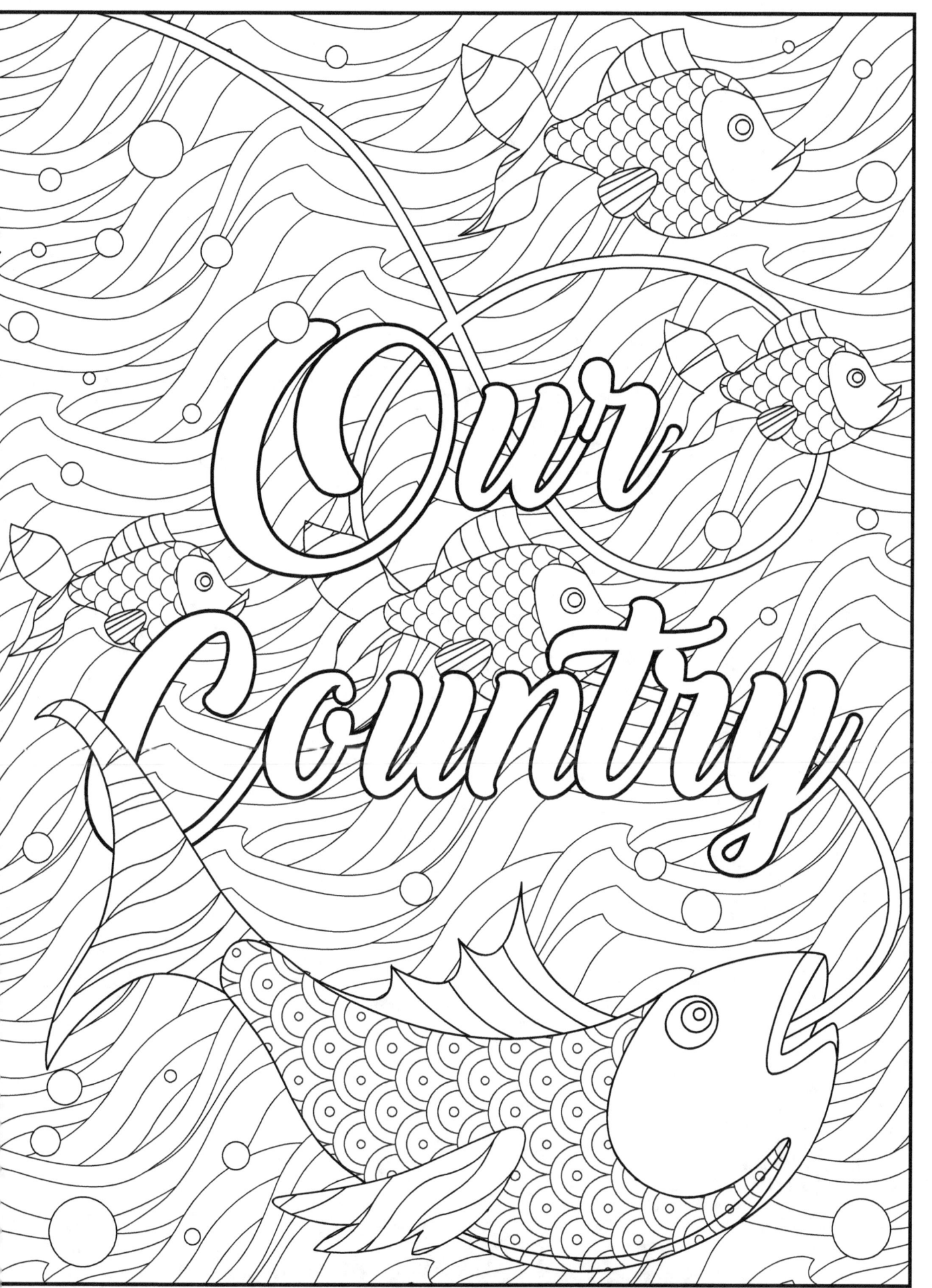

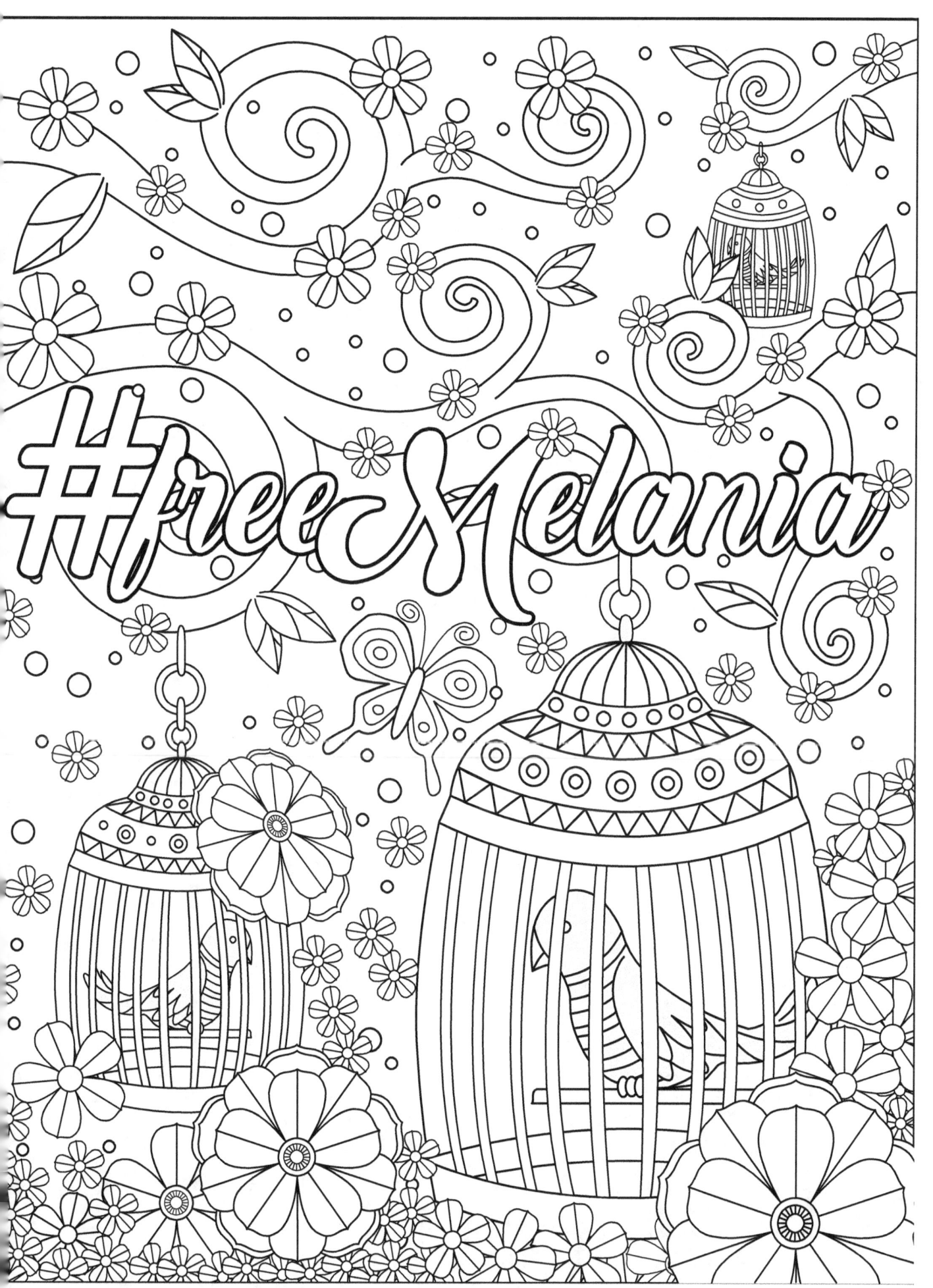

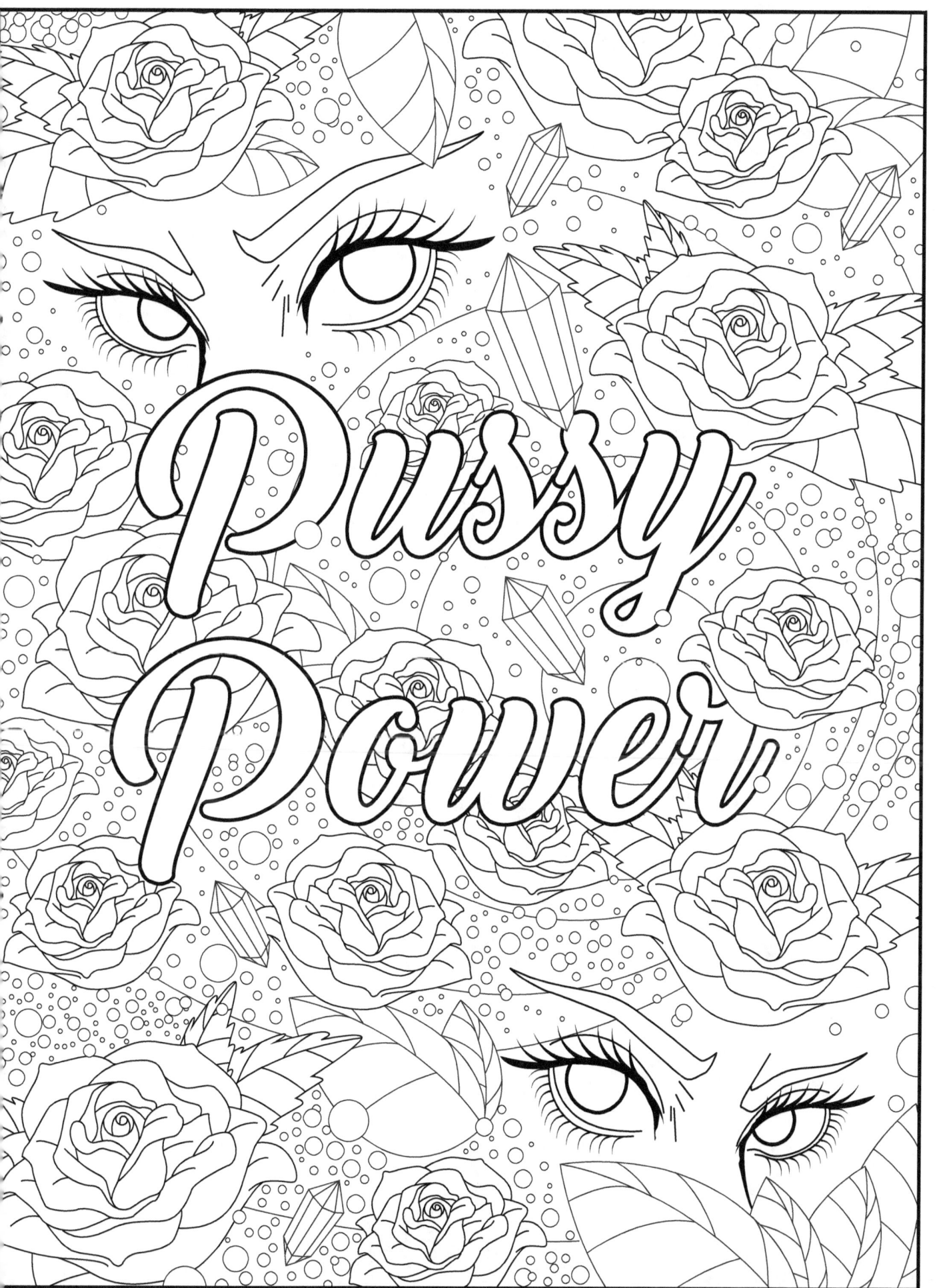

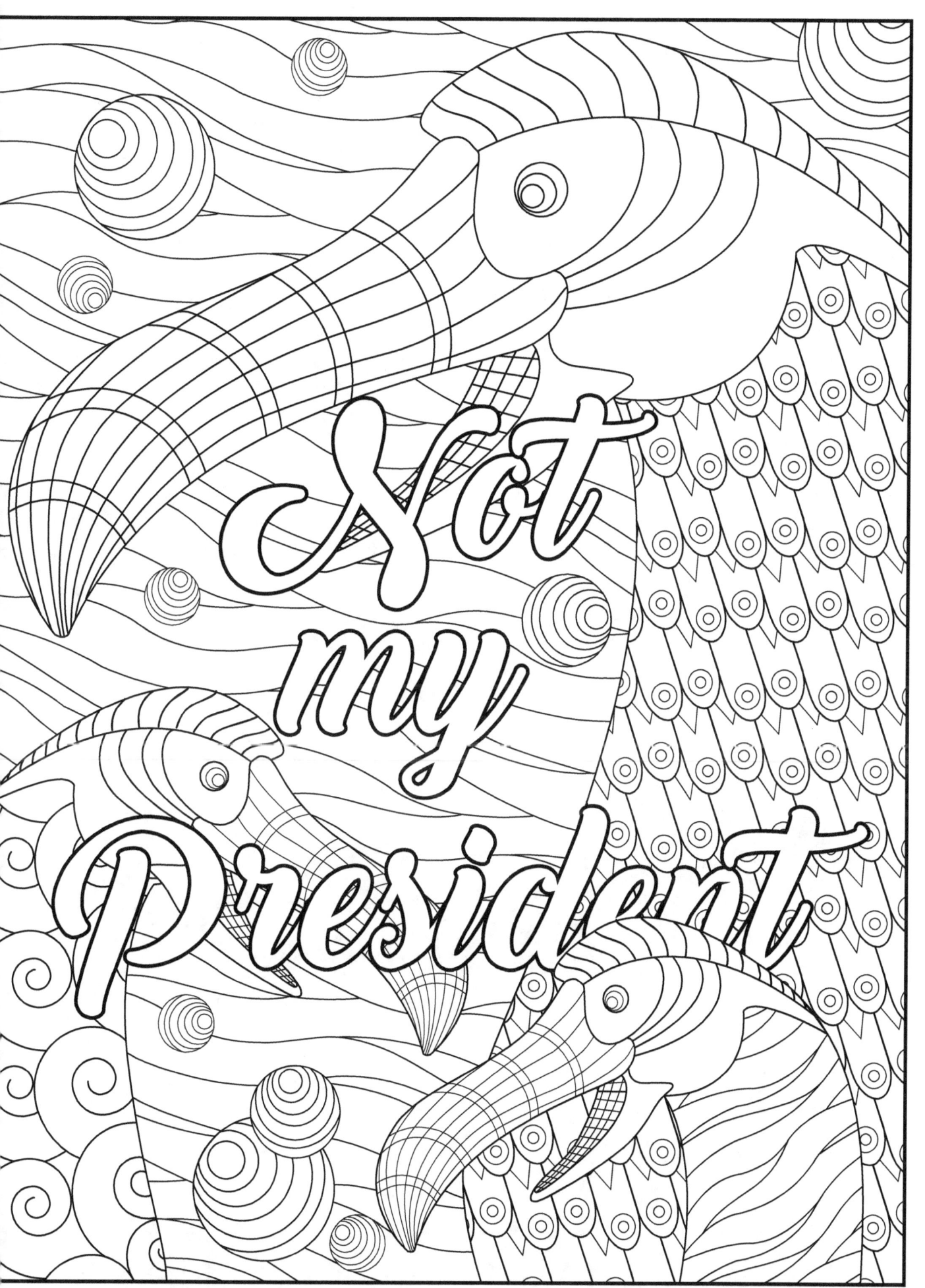

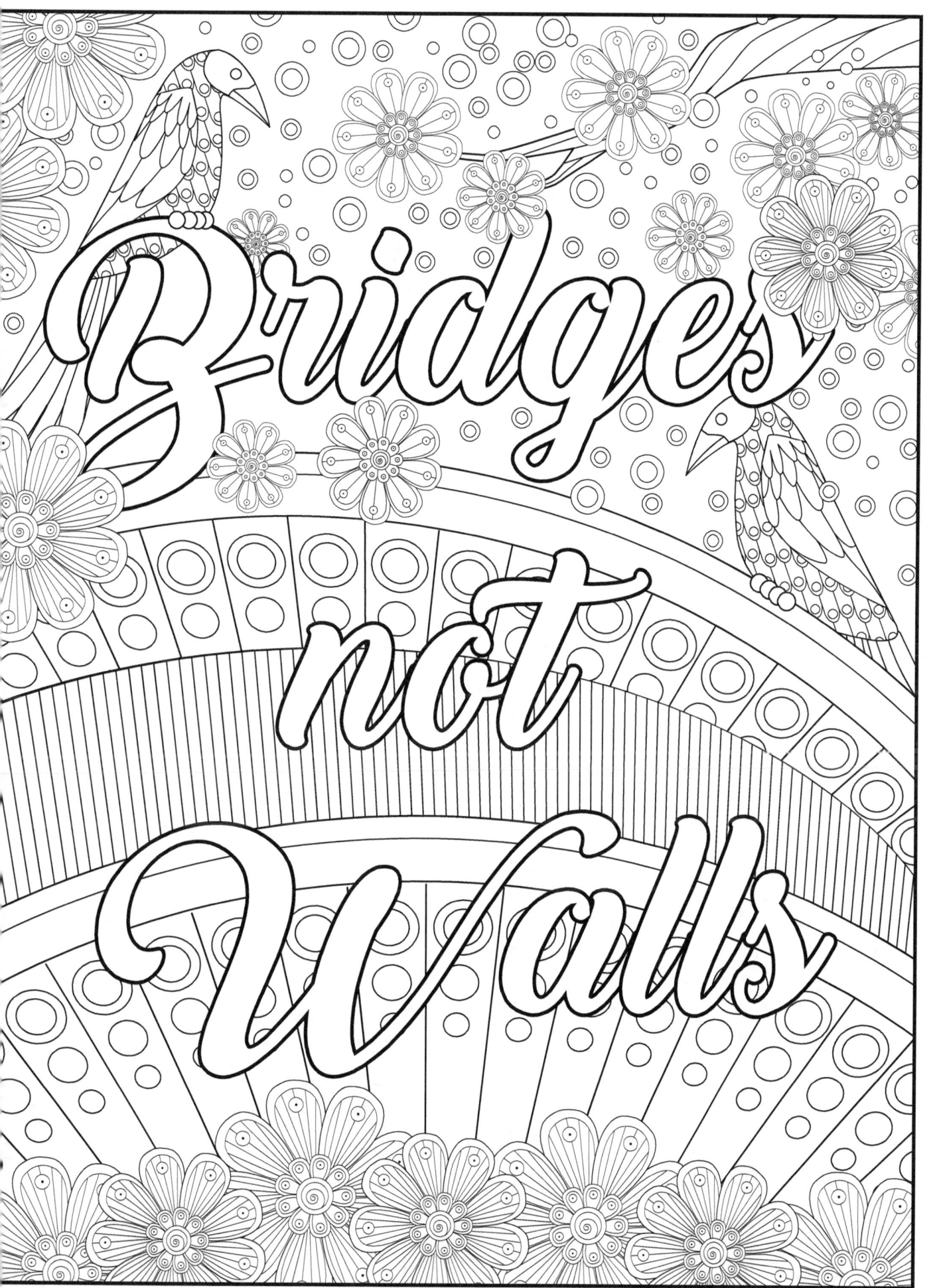

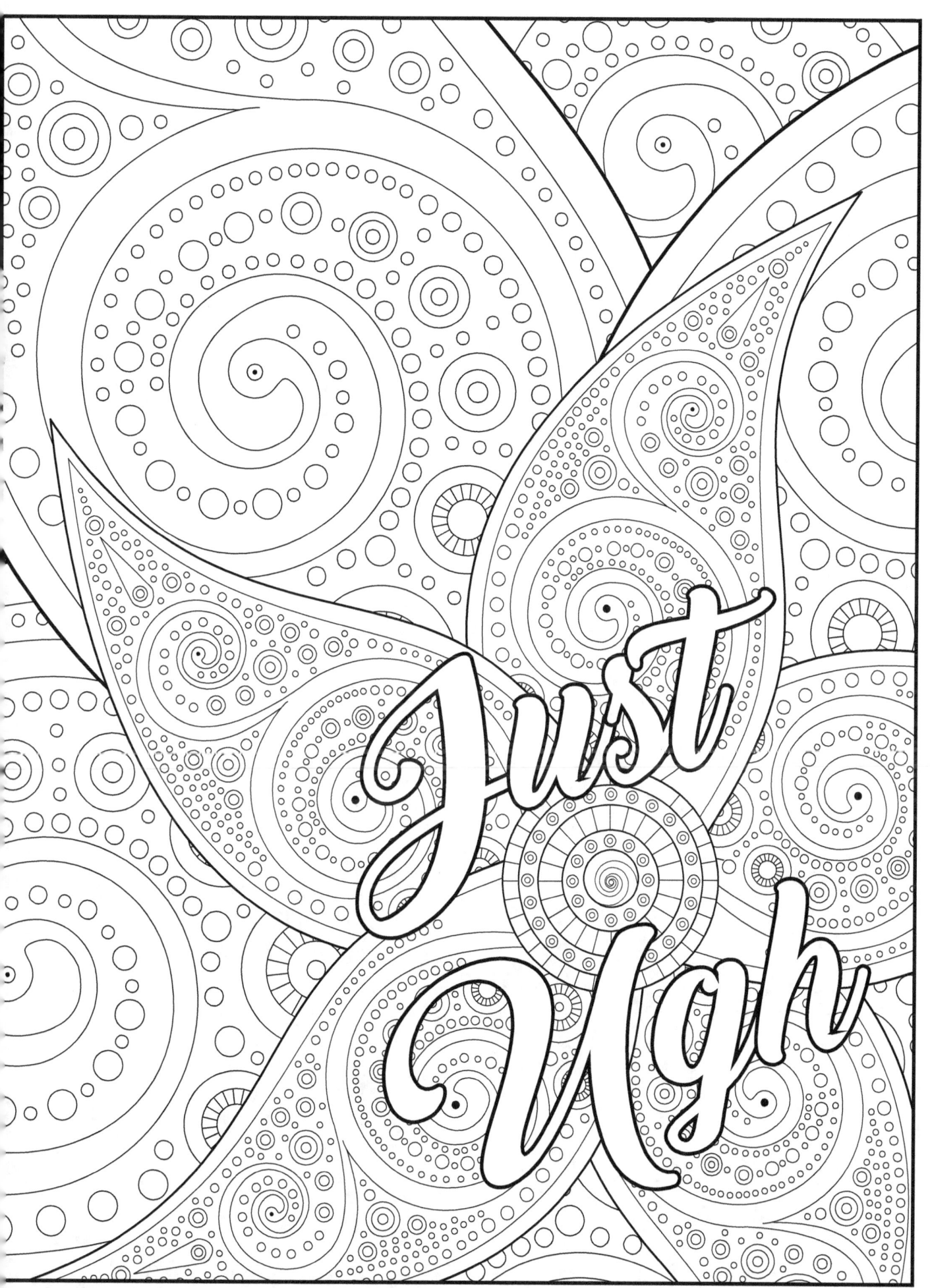

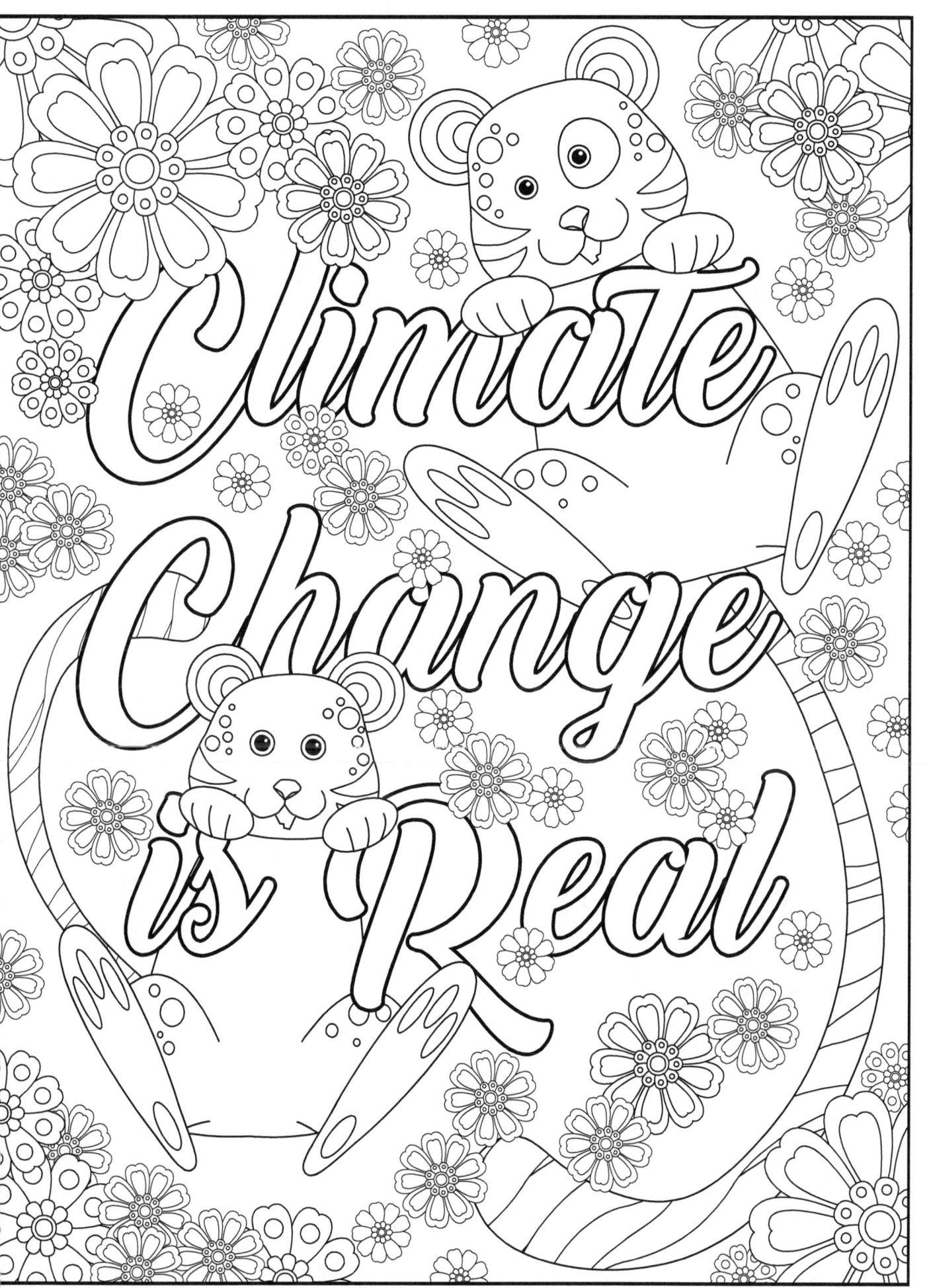

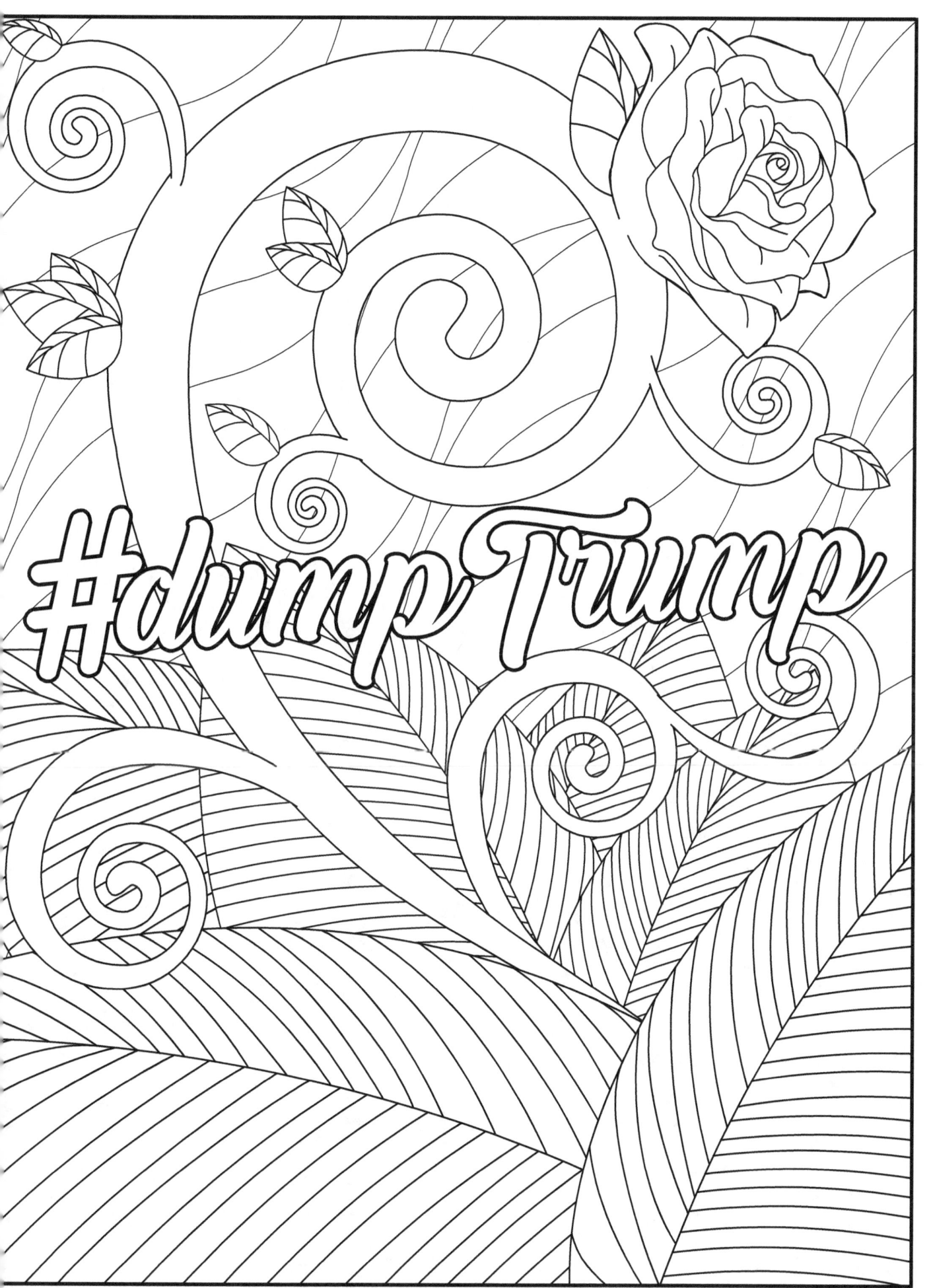

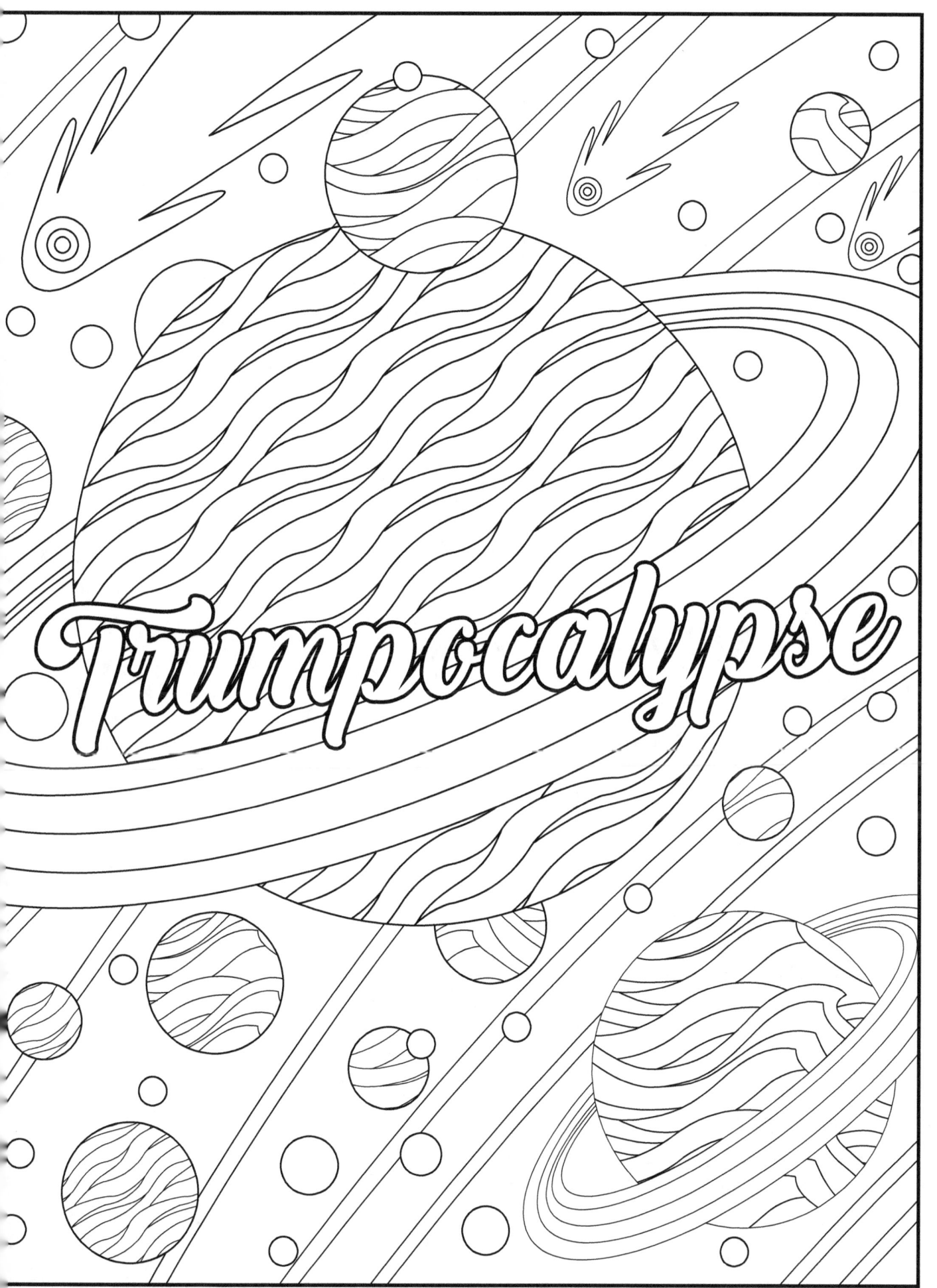

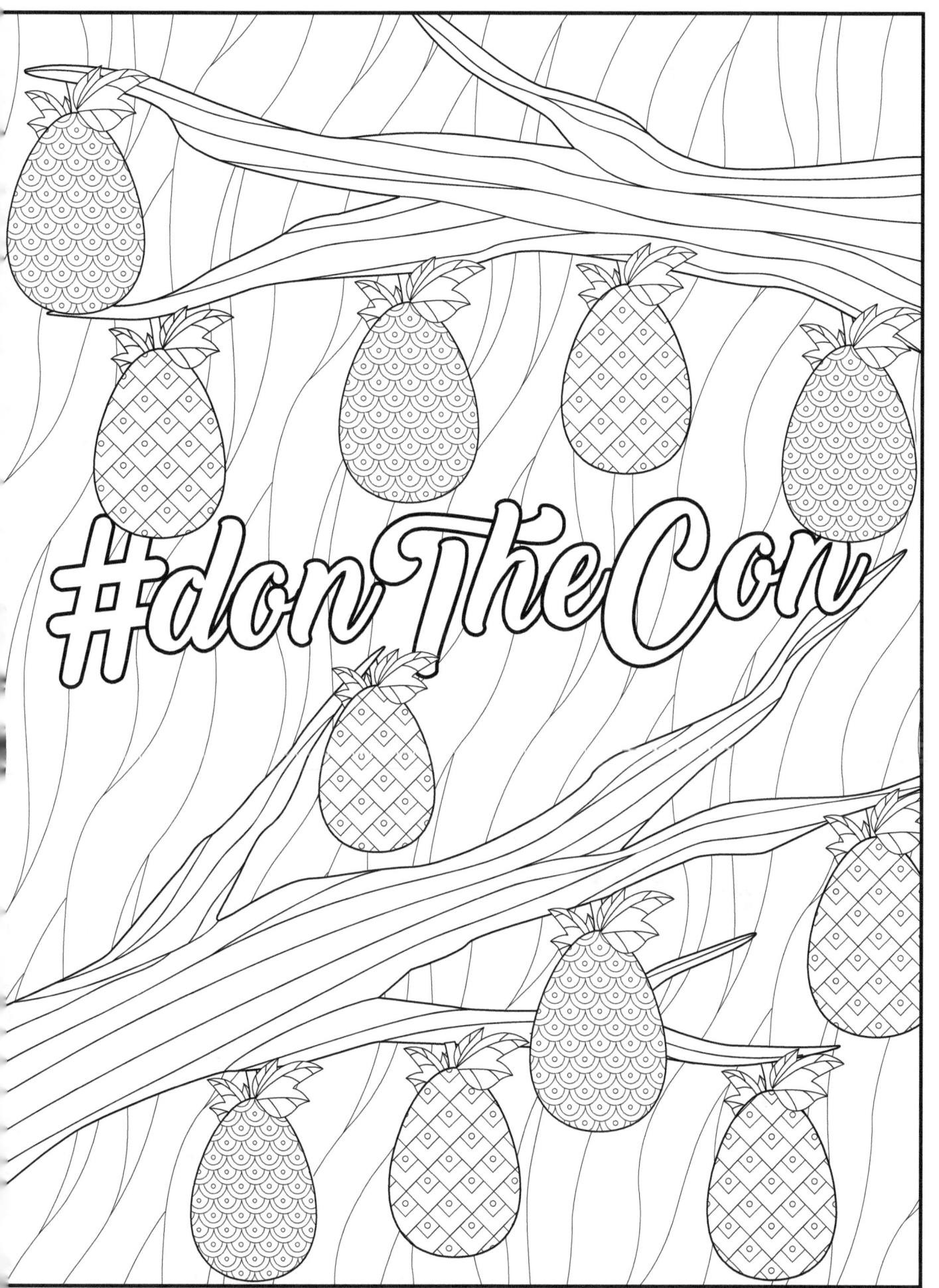

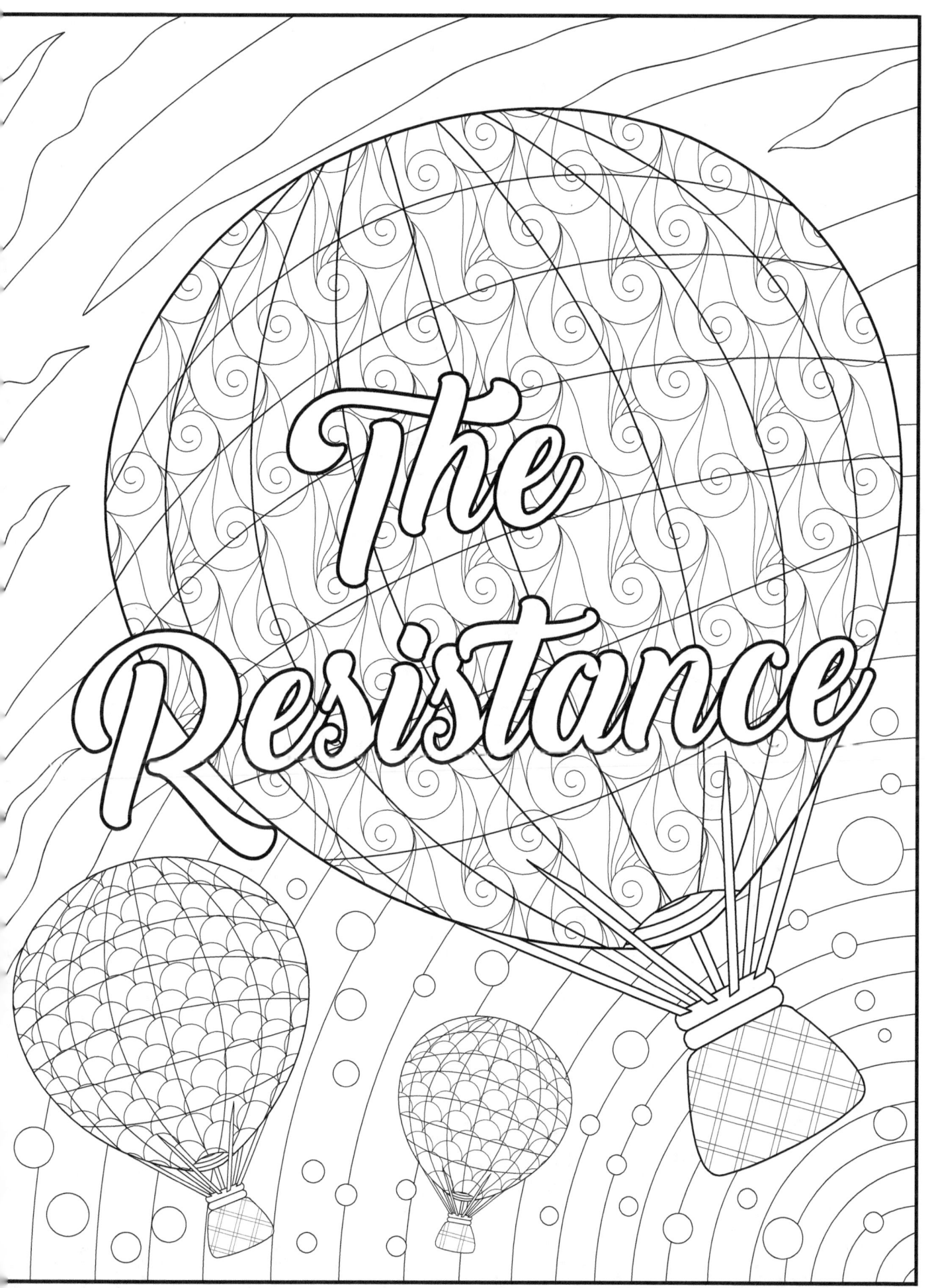

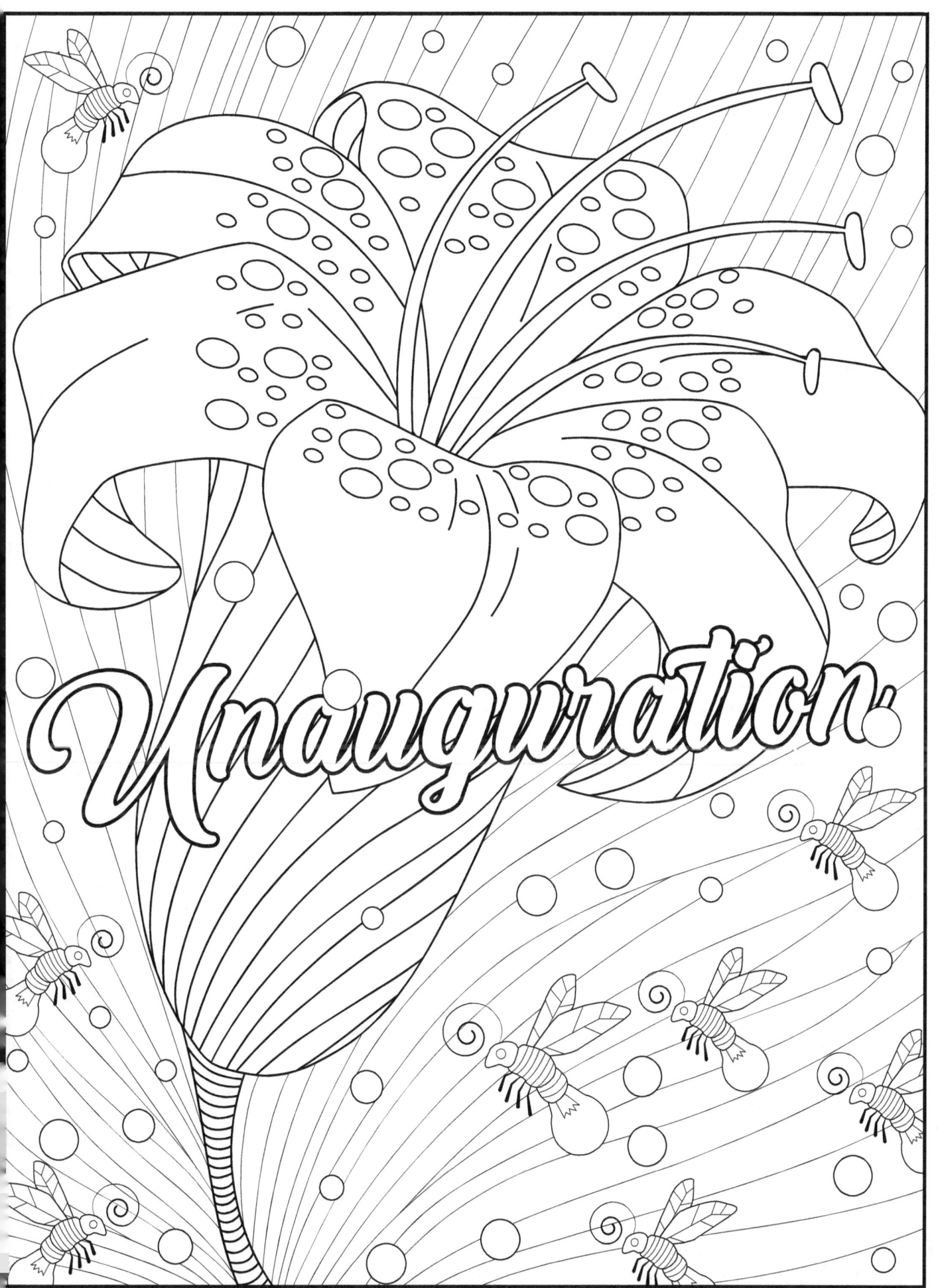

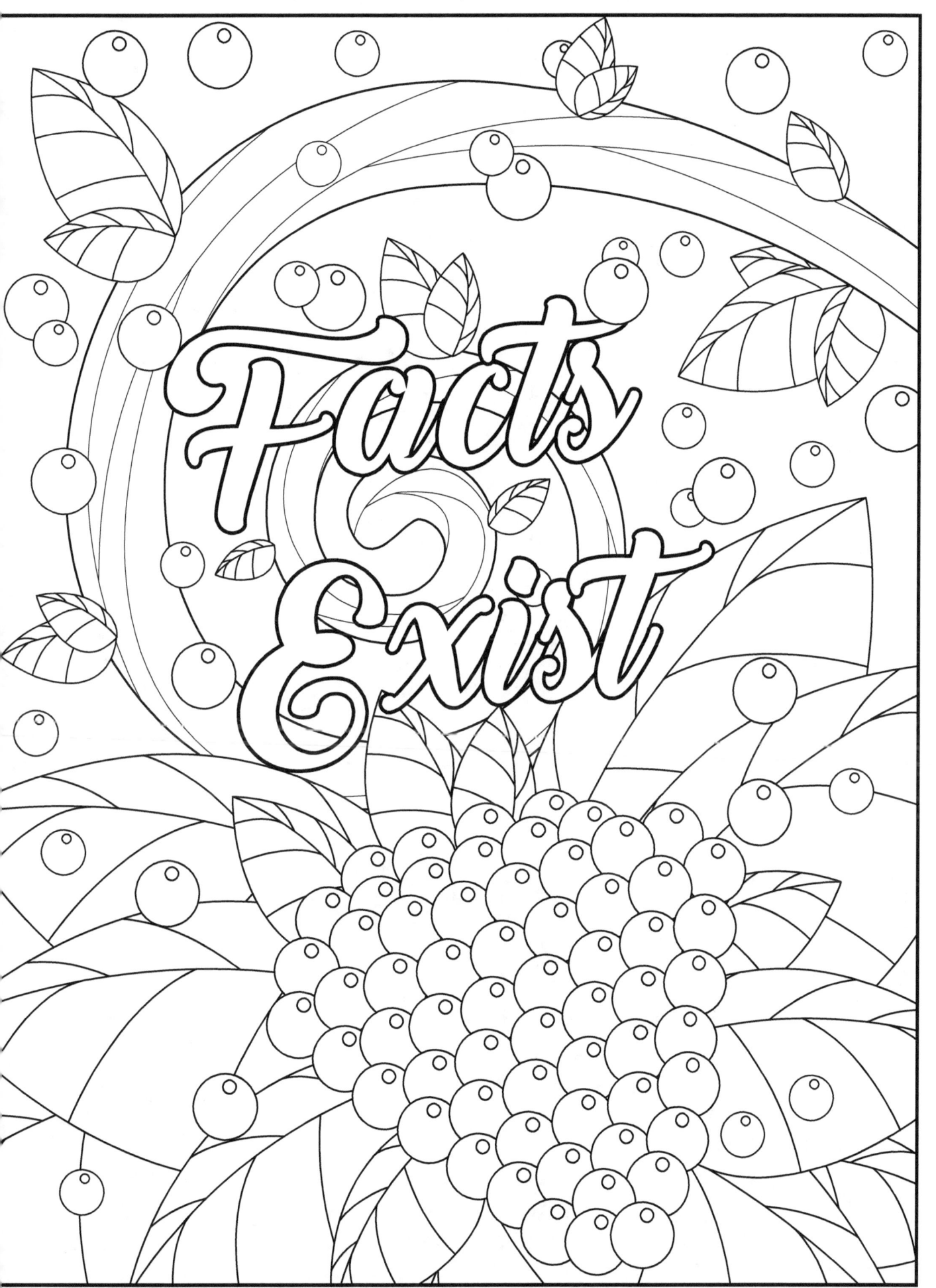

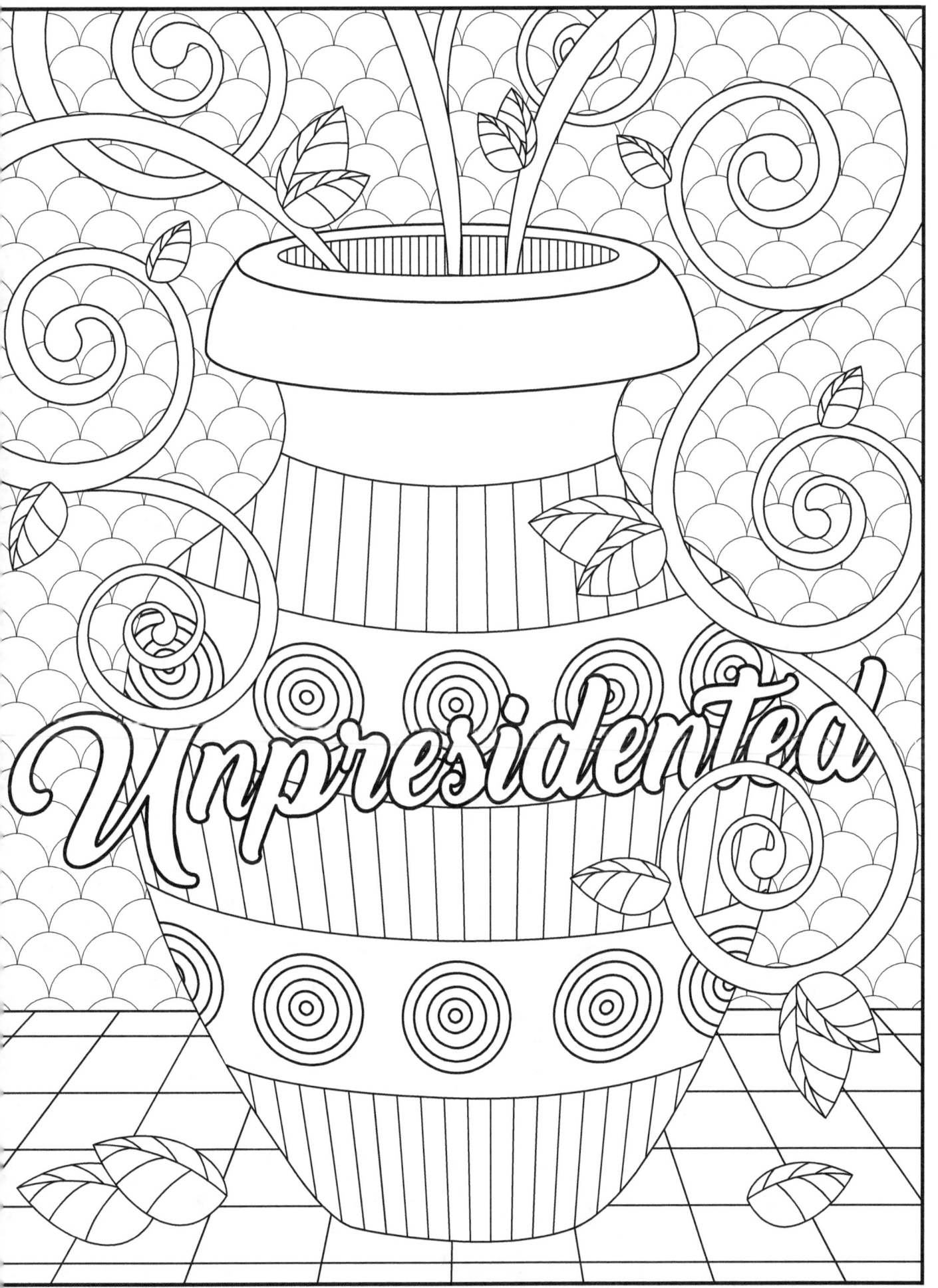

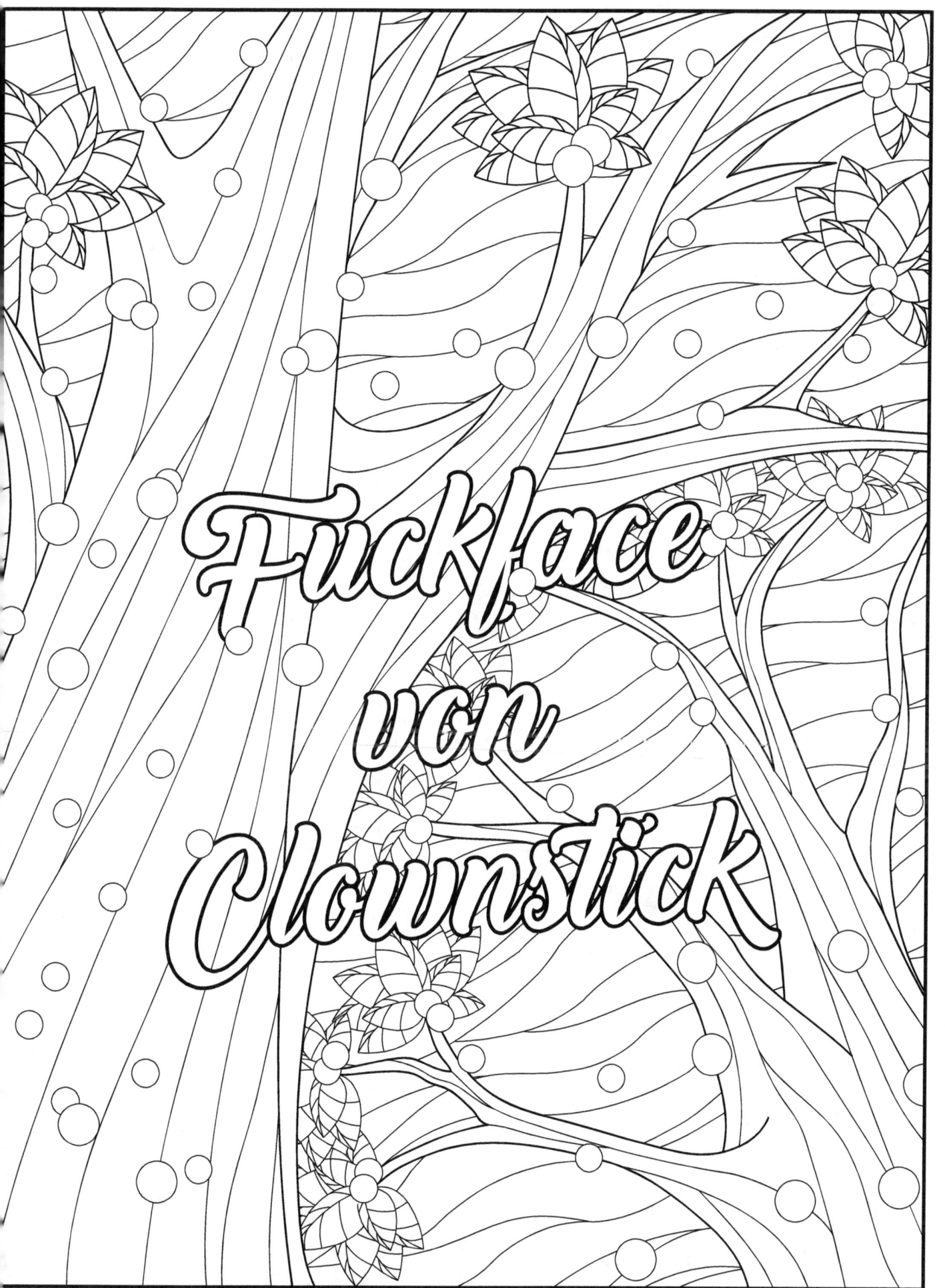

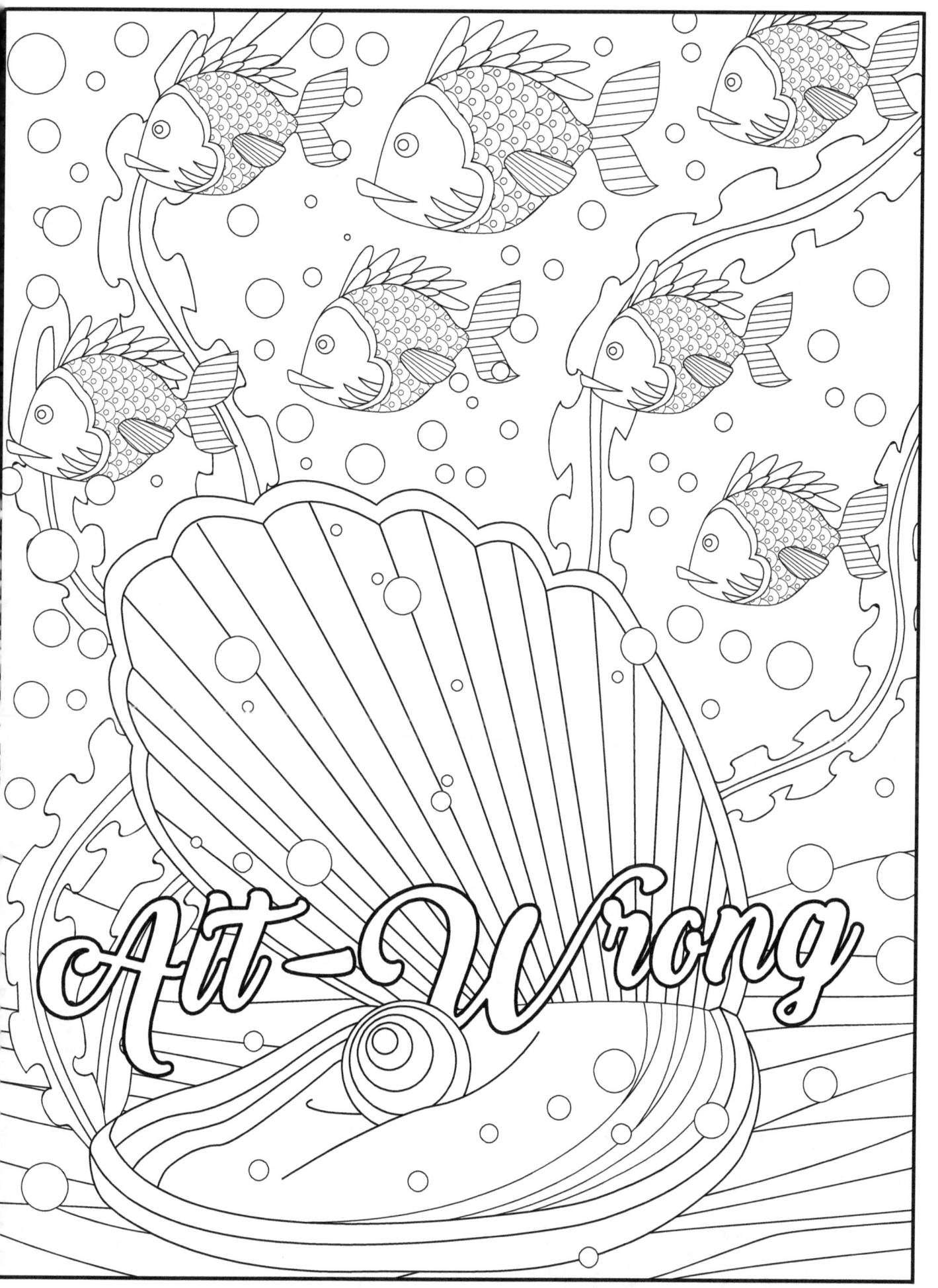

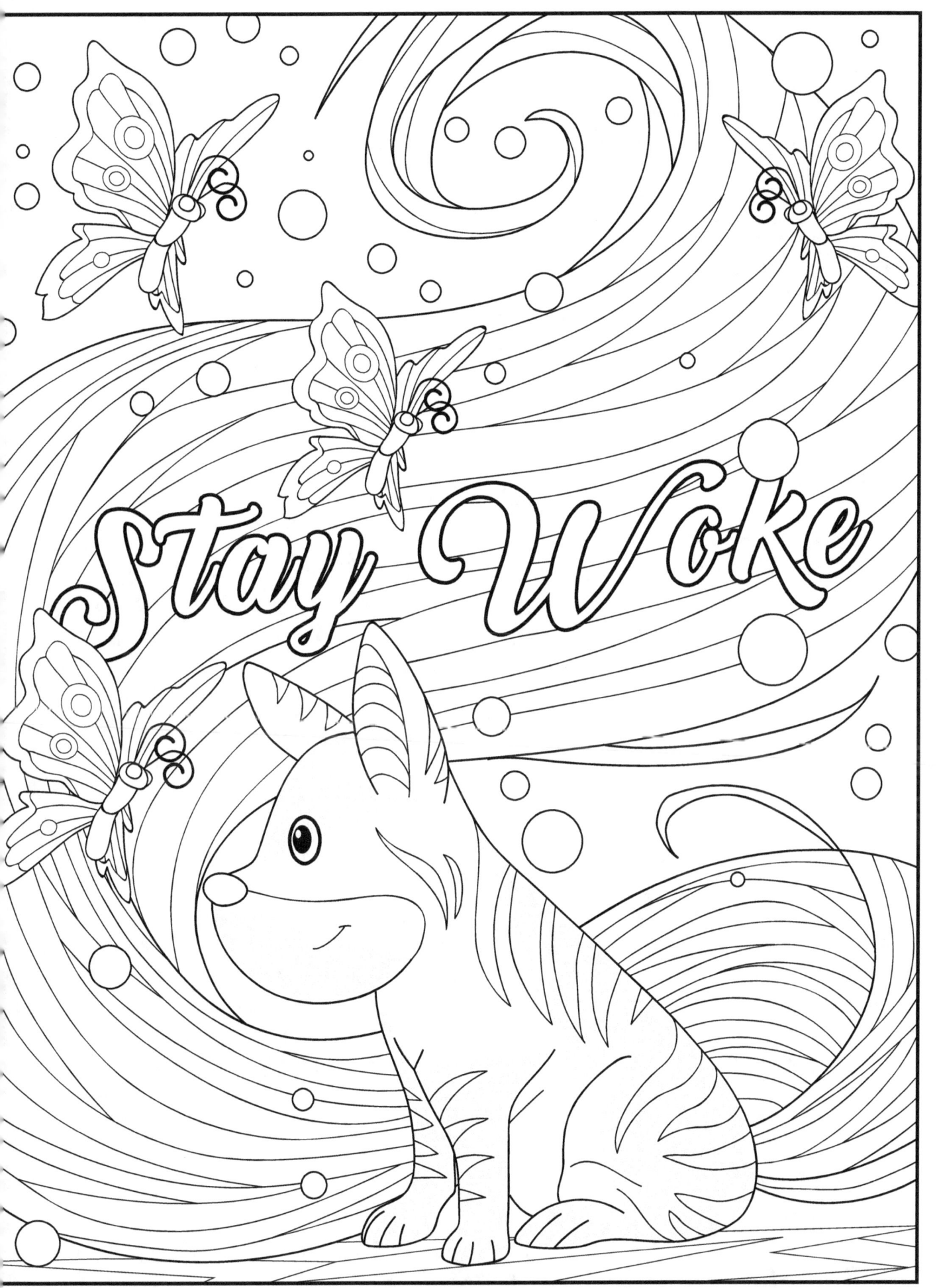

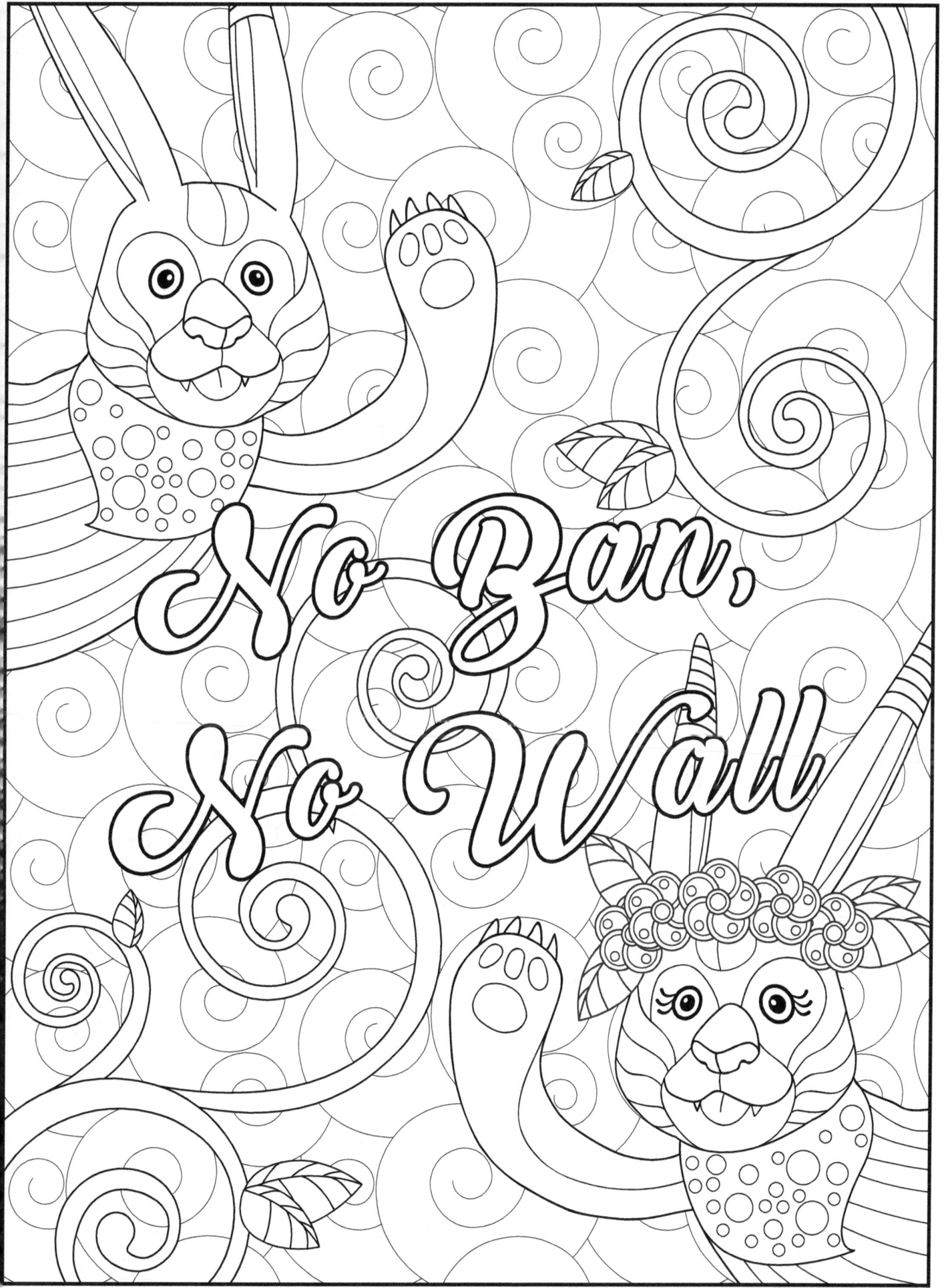

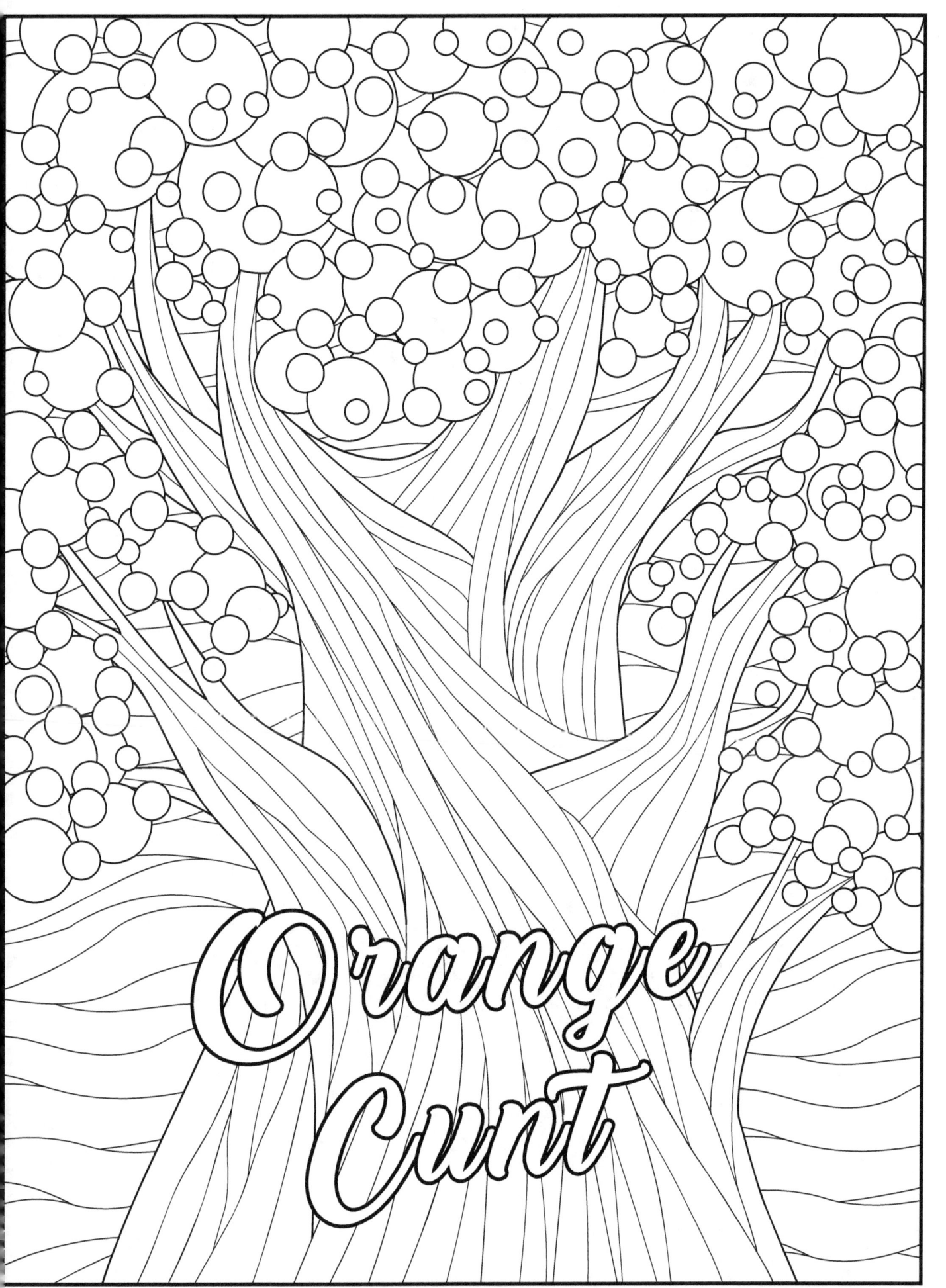

GET YOUR BONUS PAGES

Download your exclusive bonus F*ck Trump coloring pages in printable PDF format at:

nastywomancoloring.com/ftrumpbonus/

SHARE YOUR CREATION

After you've colored a particularly satisfying picture, take a photo and upload it to facebook.com/nastywomancoloring/. We'd love to see your work!

www.ingramcontent.com/pod-product-compliance
Lightning Source LLC
Chambersburg PA
CBHW081019170526
45158CB00010B/3099